Holy Moment

Revisiting the Beauty of Eden Daily

Jacy Lee Pulford

All Rights Reserved

©2024

In loving memory of Ruth,
dedicated to her beautiful flowers.
Rachel, Renée, Regan and Rylee;
Stay in the garden like she taught you.

1

Holy Moment: an encounter with the Holy God

"And the Lord God formed man of the dust of the ground, and breathed into his nostrils the breath of life; and man became a living soul. And the Lord God planted a garden eastward in Eden; and there he put the man whom he had formed." Genesis 2:7-8

Before the temple, there was a garden. It was lavished with the best of what we could feast on. God provided every morsel of goodness for the first man. He walked and talked with him, investing in a relationship that was enriching. The Lord delighted in meeting his needs. He satisfied every longing with a perfectly planned paradise where man could enjoy life and thrive unconditionally.

Gardens are visually pleasing—even a vegetable garden decorated with food that matches the colors of the rainbow. If you have time soon, just sit quietly in a garden somewhere.

Life is happening in a garden. Life has always been awake in a garden. As the rain water nourishes the soil, minerals and nutrients feed the plants that grow the tasty pollen so insects and animals can live.

God planned how gardens should be.

A place where life is found.

A place where He is present.

Sitting in the midst of a garden, we tend to ask questions to try comprehending this complicated thing called life. One question we may have is this: why would a God so pure allow the potential of unholy to dwell in His presence? The truth is that we were never meant to become unholy. We were always meant to be holy as He is holy.

We were always meant to walk in unison with our Creator, surrendering ourselves to a loving relationship as pure as He is. The Lord wanted creation to have communion. A bond that would be more beautiful than the very plants and trees planted in Eden. With a garden flowing with refreshing, clean water, full of delectable fruits to feast on, God set the table for us to sit with Him. The Lord desires our company.

If only the desire of the first man and woman was to stay in the presence of the Lord. Instead, their desire to seek satisfaction outside of the One who brings life continues to bring humanity farther from our destined resting place.

The sin of Adam and Eve is now a seed planted within our human makeup. It was sowed the moment their lips tasted of the forbidden fruit. There is potential within all of us to deny the very Father who has laid out everything we need to live and be sustained. It's a sad reality we must come to grip with.

When sin entered the garden, so did the deception of self-sufficiency. The serpent whispers to us still: *"You can be like God and do life alone."* And we have believed the slithering enemy ever since from generation to generation.

This possessed the conscience of the first couple. They believed the lie of the enemy. What was once a wonderful, holy moment changed to a scene of sorrow. It's heartbreaking. The voice of self-sufficiency pulled them right out of God's hands, and He let them go, turning them over to their own lusts and desires outside of paradise.

A gentle God doesn't force loving commitment.

The beauty of Eden was never tainted. Their unholy actions didn't change paradise. Paradise changed inside their unholy minds. What was good was no longer good. What was once enough was no longer enough. They thought God was keeping more away from them. The first man and woman were sufficient until the moment they listened to the deceiver.

Self-sufficiency was a cloud they couldn't stand on. A vapor of nothing. The enemy continues to project a foundation that's a facade, and as God's people stepped outside of paradise, their steps slid towards the gates of hell.

Eden was created on solid ground, but when we feel self-sufficient, it's a mirage that captures the souls meant to glorify the Father. It will snatch us from where we were always meant to be: in the presence of the Lord Jesus Christ.

God still desires that Holy Moment in the garden where His children rest in the fruits of His provision under His wing and protection. A place where we are basking in the glow of His Spirit, satisfied with Him. Where rich conversation is had throughout the seconds of a day. Where relationship between creation and Creator is intimately woven together like a strong tapestry.

If you're ever curious why devotion is important, this is your reason.

Devotion is investing our time, energy, and purpose to the Lord. It's an invitation to revisit the first garden and experience the beauty of Eden. To have full dependency on a God who provides and deeply loves. A place of peace and refuge.

Eden was the sanctuary before a sanctuary was ever built. It was bliss created by God's hands as a place of solitude. He satisfied their senses with good fruit to taste, good conversation to hear, good flowers to see, good fragrances to smell, and good grass to touch. Eden was a good place.

That is why they had to leave. They no longer saw it as good. Their sin perverted their perspective and twisted their thinking. Adam and Eve no longer honored paradise. They no longer honored what God said was good. Yet in His Holy love and mercy, our Almighty Creator became the Savior from sin and death as He gave His life on the cross at Calvary to reverse the curse over mankind and to reconcile His children back to where they belong.

With Jesus in a new Garden experience.

Today, we are given grace to approach the goodness of Eden and have every need met yet again through daily devotion. This means reading the Word, having an active prayer life, using our expression and service as worship, to sing praise, and the sacrifice of fasting so our flesh submits back to God.

When we connect with God through devotion, we are given the key back to Eden in a beautiful new way. A secret Garden like no other. The secret place of the Most High.

"He that dwelleth in the secret place of the most High shall abide under the shadow of the Almighty." Psalm 91:1

We often don't give Eden a thought anymore. It's as if when Adam and Eve left the garden, so did we—spiritually speaking. We see it as a paradise that no longer exists. But the Lord has challenged me in a beautiful way recently.

The challenge that maybe when I approach Him through devotion each day, the gates to Eden are once again open, and I am able to stroll with God in the midst of paradise. *Just as He intended.* Where the location isn't the focus, but He is. A supernatural experience that can't be compared.

Calvary happened to defeat death and sin once and for all. We know this. We've been taught this. We believe this. Yet with God, there's always more. Jesus dying on the cross tore the veil, bringing us endless opportunities to have Holy Moments. Bringing us back to Eden redeemed and refreshed in the presence of our Father.

I can't wait for the day I see Jesus on His Throne in Heaven. Wanting to be there is a good thing. It's a place of power and strength.

But it's not the only place to find God.

The Throne is where you can worship Him. But the Garden is where you can walk with Him.

Devotion with God is devoting time to spend with God, but self-sufficiency says we don't have the time. It whispers idolatrous frameworks that we can make it through the day without Him. It's as though we ourselves have become as gods, trying to spend our time with everyone and everything, our phones mirroring the illusion of omnipresence while the God who gave us time in the first place patiently waits in a spiritual Garden full of all we could ever need.

Time stands still in Eden with the Lord Jesus Christ. How beautiful of a place where we can have a real relationship with our Great Creator. What paradise! Where Holy meets with unholy. *Fear isn't in charge. Worry is meaningless. Brokenness is mended. Tears will reap future joy.*

That's the promise of Eden. You can bring your cares to God in the Garden, and He'll take care of them for you. Where your weeping isn't for nothing. Your sorrow waters the seeds that will eventually become edible fruit that's approved.

The Father comforts His child and gives you a promise of better days. Every step He watches and guides. There will never be a place where you arrive that God has not been before. Even in the new moments, God was there first.

I can't believe my Creator wants to spend time with me. He wants to talk and walk with me.

In the grace of His love, the Lord pours out every good thing to those willing and obedient. We must make time for the Holy Moment. That responsibility is a gift to us—that we may carve out time to communicate with our Lord.

The same way that God assigned Adam a job in the garden, He assigns one to us, not to forsake the beauty of a Holy Moment with Jesus. It's when unholy people connect with a Holy God during personal devotion time—a moment out of our busy day to walk the garden with God to share our deep concerns, wildest dreams, and most importantly, to listen to His soothing words, soaking up the sweet presence of the Comforter and refreshing the dry well within our hearts that can only be filled by the Living Water. Holy Moments aren't reserved for only morning or night. It's any time we set aside to abide with God.

"For the Lord shall comfort Zion: he will comfort all her waste places; and he will make her wilderness like Eden, and her desert like the garden of the Lord; joy and gladness shall be found therein, thanksgiving, and the voice of melody." Isaiah 51:3

If a Holy Moment is important and essential, why do we choose to stay outside of the garden? The Lord began to bring to my mind a very sad and dangerous fact concerning His children who claim to live by faith.

Many don't live by a refreshed, personal faith.

Most of us, in our busyness and complacent self-sufficiency, live by *old* faith. Stale faith. Trying to build families, ministries, churches on faith that has not been carried back to the garden with God.

Adam and Eve no longer have access to the garden, but we do. Through the sin offering of the precious blood of the Lord Jesus Christ, there's a way back into this lovely, secret garden. When we place our self-sufficiency at the feet of the cross, the gate is opened, and Jesus calls us in with joy.

Be aware. The serpent still slithers among the people of God, whispering ways we can depend on our own unholy fragility. As the first man and woman forgot whom they belonged to, so do we. We forget we are not our own. That we did not make ourselves.

The entire Universe was crafted in the hands of a God who is the only One who saves. However, we have demoted the Lord from Creator to assistant, waving when we are in an emergency. The sidekick to our imaginative superhero fantasies.

Devotion requires a sacrifice of our comfort, but we have penciled God into our schedules out of convenience rather than communion. The reality is, like Adam and Eve, our vision is on the fruit we were not meant to eat, starving our spirit of the nourishment found in a Holy Moment *where God becomes enough.*

The downfall of humanity was when we believed we could sustain ourselves without the Lord's provision. It was in the garden where temptation found Adam and Eve. At the same time, in the garden was also where the Solution was that would help them overcome the temptation.

You will face challenges as you begin to make time for a Holy Moment with God or even as you are dwelling in it.

The garden is paradise, but our minds are not.

Thankfully, Jesus is the Solution to every temptation. He wants to be with you through it all. So He waits for an invitation.

The concept of a Holy Moment came to my heart a few years ago. It's been a truth I've chewed on alone for a long time and only have briefly shared. I began to realize the significance of this idea and the chains that could be broken in the mindsets we've adopted about daily devotion time with God.

If we can grasp the magnitude of personal devotion time with the Lord, it would change the world as we see it. Our eyes will become like God's eyes. Our hearts will be tender like His. Our overall vision will mirror the vision of God as we navigate the hard and rough places of life. A hope will rise within us. A sure foundation will settle before us.

Hopefully as you read this book, you'll be willing to bring any self-sufficient motives to the cross to die and to be buried with Jesus in the grave. While the Eden in Genesis was a spot on the map, we can now enter Eden in the spot where we kneel.

On the rug. At your bedside. In a dark bathroom tucked in the back of your home. While you rock the baby in the middle of the night or in a corporate lunch room under fluorescent lighting.

If we turn our hearts to connecting with the Lord God Almighty in our ordinary, He will be there.

Unholy abiding Holy, walking side by side. Once again.

2

The more that I think about this concept, the idea that we can revisit the solitude of Eden during our daily devotion, the more in awe I am of our God. His ways are undoubtedly perfect.

Right now, I'm sitting in bed with my laptop, watching our youngest son stretch and rest next to the family dog. The weather report said snow, but once again, it's just a cold rain in January. Our oldest son has already finished his chores and is enjoying his reward. This is how most mornings are for us. Nothing exciting, and yet, the most blessed life.

To think that in the middle of the ordinary I have access to a Holy Moment with God is incredibly beautiful. And also very humbling. Our Creator became the sacrifice for sin and is the key to unlock Holy Moments in our every day.

God wants me—with a frizzy, messy bun and worn-in robe. A person who has fallen more times than she'd like to admit. Whose patience is often on the rocks, maternal worries tucked under her sleeve, and socks that never properly stay on her feet. *Yet God wants me.*

I guess that's the thing about God. Those things, compared to the bigger picture, don't matter much. It's the heart He wants. It's the relationship with His creation. While the rest of what the Lord has created doesn't have the choice to serve Him, since all nature automatically bows down, we are different.

We're given a choice. To serve God or not.

The Lord knew that forced love isn't really love at all. He desires something more meaningful. The thought of knowing that right here—in the middle of my ruffled, spotted comforter full of dog hair—I can kneel at the feet of Jesus is powerful. I don't need to leave my house. *He is right here!*

I don't need to follow a ritualistic list to make sure I'm clean enough to enter into His presence. I'm accepted. To freely be with God, in a Holy Moment, among an ordinary stage. A miracle among the mundane. Where He gets all the glory.

I'm reminded of Mary giving birth in that Bethlehem stable. There was nothing special about it. The structure wasn't gold plated or bejewelled. It was Jesus that made it special.

"And she brought forth her firstborn son, and wrapped him in swaddling clothes, and laid him in a manger; because there was no room for them in the inn." Luke 2:7

Many times we think the circumstances and the atmosphere need to be perfect, or close to it, in order for God to meet with us. Yet when the Lord Jesus Christ was born, the environment wasn't ideal. He could have come as a majestic king dressed in fine linens, manifested behind castle walls, sitting on a golden throne behind a guarded door.

However, that wouldn't align with God's purpose: to be known. How can we know someone well at a distance? It's difficult to do that without consistent interaction. The heart of God is never to be so far away from our reach. So, the Lord came in a way anyone could have access to Him. That's how lives were changed.

It was truly a Holy Moment when the exhausted Mary and Joseph saw the Savior enter the world through the not-so-glamorous process of childbirth. Dingy hay under their feet, sweat beads across their foreheads, no crowd to cheer them on. Maybe a little huff from a curious animal nearby. The grime of travel still on their skin. The absence of a sterile hospital with nurses swarming the room every hour to check the mother's vitals. There were no beeping monitors tracking the health of baby Jesus. In the dark of the night without the intervention of comfort, *Jesus came.*

And He still arrives that way to us now.

In those moments where the comfort and the conveniences of life have faded away, we often feel so far from the Lord. We tell ourselves, *"This isn't the ideal environment for God to show."* As if that ever stopped Him before. A disgusting stable in the middle of a small town, surrounded by nothing but filthy animals, isn't the ideal environment for a baby to be born, especially a baby who is the King. Yet that's how Jesus works.

He enters into the most dirty, uncomfortable places despite its cleanliness or proper location, knowing full well unholy can't taint Holy. The moment Jesus enters into any space, His presence overcomes the presence of anything else.

"And the angel of the Lord said unto her, Behold, thou art with child, and shalt bear a son, and shalt call his name Ishmael; because the Lord hath heard thy affliction." Genesis 16:11

Hagar faithfully served the household of Abram and Sarai who will be known as Abraham and Sarah. She had been thrown into their marital hurdle in their attempt to have a child, and she had no control. Hagar was harshly dealt with and treated terribly by no fault of her own. So, she fled from comfort in search of refuge and relief.

Hagar left the place she called home and the people she thought she could trust. The selfishness of Sarai and Abram casted a shadow over Hagar's life, and she could not take it anymore. It was in the wilderness by a fountain that the angel of the Lord found Hagar. Among the unkempt trees, she was there, and He met with her. It wasn't an ideal place for God to show up. Where we are almost never is.

I've always wondered if Hagar was in the middle of travailing prayer when God showed up, but the Bible doesn't say. In fact, she could have been weary both from her journey and her worry. If she uttered any words at all, they were probably not eloquent or delivered with poise. Imagine the emotions that stirred within Hagar's heart. She had been faithful yet treated like property. She was a good servant and yet still didn't earn the approval of Sarai. I imagine the weight on Hagar's shoulders felt extremely heavy as she collapsed by the fountain, no longer able to carry on.

Scripture tells us that the Lord knew what Hagar was going through. The Lord told her of the promise upon her unborn son Ishmael. That the reason for this blessing was because *"the Lord hath heard thy affliction."* Hagar, unfairly misused, was seen by her Heavenly Father. What's more, the Lord wanted her to know it. That she was in His thoughts. In this part of the story, affliction means depression, misery, and trouble. It's more than just pain. It's a state of heaviness that consumes someone's life.

God was telling Hagar that even though this wasn't ideal, He was there. This wasn't convenient, comfortable, justified…but He would take care of her anyway. The Holy Moment between the Lord and Hagar didn't happen in the cozy warmth of a home. It took place out of her element in the middle of the mess and wilderness.

The first time the angel of the Lord appeared to a person on record in the scripture, it was to an overwhelmed woman who was rejected and uncertain about her future. If God can meet with Hagar in the wilderness, He doesn't need the environment to be perfect.

He just needs a moment of your time.

Maybe it's our Western culture or the current church culture. We tend to think the right lighting, the right song, or the right decorations will create the right environment for God to work.

I get that. I believe we should do our best to prepare the atmosphere as we invite the Spirit of the Lord to move. Then again, will we be okay with Him showing up when everything is not ideal? Do we truly believe God can be in the middle of our mess because He just wants to be known?

When we are living day-by-day, it can be hard to show up and give God our time. There are many things on our to-do lists. The needs of others beg for our attention. Our expectations looming in the forefront of our weary minds.

My prayer for us is that we will show up anyway. That the idea of having an ideal environment won't stop us from coming to God. Not letting the expectation of the perfectly crafted prayer hinder our words. That we may realize devotion to Jesus isn't activated by a checklist or even the most powerful worship song. Devotion is activated by our humility, bringing our unholiness to the altar in all its disorderliness.

It is true. God wants us to bring our best. At the same time, it is also true that God also wants us to bring our mess. Two things can be true at once. He will take it all. God wants our hearts.

"Thereafter, Hagar used another name to refer to the Lord, who had spoken to her. She said, "You are the God who sees me." She also said, "Have I truly seen the One who sees me?" Genesis 16:13 NLT

In beautiful disbelief, Hagar couldn't believe the Lord of all the earth had seen her! She was able to return to a difficult situation with a promise: *that her God was watching*. The trial Hagar was going through had to run its course. Only this time, she knew Who was by her side. God saw her and will continue to see her always. What a beautiful revelation!

How amazing is our Lord? He is still the God who sees! He sees me, and He sees you right where we are. Imperfectly here.

God sees our families. Our friends. Our co-workers. Our pastors.

God sees our pain. Our tears. Our fears. Our worries. Our struggles.

God sees our dreams. Our goals. Our plans. Our full desires.

God knows that a Holy Moment is how to build a Holy Relationship. Hagar was returning home with new knowledge about her Lord. He did not completely remove her situation but gave her a gift of revelation that built her faith.

Most of us want the obstacle or the issue that's holding us down to be removed. To be fair, sometimes He does do that. However, more often than not, God reveals to us another piece of who He is so that we can withstand the storm.

The Lord saw Hagar when she really needed to be seen. It didn't matter what the future held. God held her future. We need to remember this. He sees us. We don't have to prepare the perfect place for Him to work in. He can do anything, anywhere. There is nothing we're going through right now that God can't use to bring glory to Himself and to connect with us in the process.

The paradise of Eden was the ideal environment. There was nothing about their surroundings that would hinder God to move. Yet the first man and woman still forgot God was there. They were still blinded that God saw them. The solitude of Eden was only made possible through the powerful hands of God.

In life, the solitude we need can't be crafted by our own hands. It will be in His alone as He sees our needs and meets with us where we are. Whether it's in the center of a laundry pile, the midnight hour as you cuddle a child for the night, or in your car on a work lunch break.

It's not the room or the environment that determines where God can show up. It's the invitation of a humble heart.

A Holy Moment can happen anywhere.

3

As I sit to write about what I feel God has given me, sometimes the words don't come easily. Normally, I'm not without words. Just ask literally anybody who knows me. My mom shares the story of how I would talk so much and have crazy energy, and to help me (and, let's be honest, herself) she gave me paper, crayons, and an old electric typewriter. Now, here I am. *Look, mom! It worked!*

There is a point in every book project where the words just don't flow. It can be frustrating and disheartening. I shared these feelings with Jen, my sweet friend who is excited about this book. She's also a creative Christian. So, I was honest with her.

I was feeling discouraged. There I was, trying to write a book about unholy meeting Holy, and I couldn't write the words. I confessed with shame how I'm supposed to be a writer. Right?

How embarrassing when a writer has no more words left! I felt stuck.

I confessed this to Jen. The words weren't coming together as "easily" as I had thought or had hoped. The process wasn't what I envisioned. Talk about vulnerability! What is it about sharing that's absolutely terrifying? Is it because of our past rejection? In a conversation of fellowship and edification, Jen spoke these true, life-giving words:

"What you're struggling with is exactly what your book is about. You don't have to strive to get the words. You just have to be with Him. He's got this book already written!"

Wow, God. I was trying to write the witty words on my own. You know. Those catch phrases that are plastered all over shirts and Instagram posts. The words that would capture someone's attention like a flashy commercial on TV. The words that would pull heart strings and make people commit to things and change lives.

I was trying to write Holy words through an unholy mindset. I was trying to write words without Jesus.

When we come to the end of ourselves, it's not the end at all. It's actually the beginning of the most beautiful relationship we will ever encounter. The most precious gift ever given.

It's the beginning of a life laid out by a Father who knows His children. Who knows what they need because they were carefully formed in the womb. *A God who is good and Holy.* When we are encountering a Holy Moment, it is only Holy because of Who is with us.

Without God, it's a moment without substance.

This is how we establish churches with no conviction and saints with traditional religion over relationship. This is how we have people who claim they know God but never seek Him outside of scheduled services. They never speak to Him. Never fully know Him.

God forbid.

God forbid that we claim to know Jesus only with our conversations with others outside of the Throne room. Where we have all the words but not the heart. Where we have taken the gospel out of the Garden where it all started, not fully understanding that in order to serve God, we must know Him, intimately seeking Him with our whole heart.

It's a dangerous thing for us to have our Christian life as a mask we wear around other people to appear close with Christ, yet He's asking, *"Who are you?"*

We can't develop close relationships without spending time and investing in the lives of people. No marriage can last if the spouses don't talk and connect. True friendships won't be developed. This is the same with the Lord. It's hypocritical to claim to know Him in public when we have yet to make an altar at home.

This is the dilemma, isn't it? To put into action what we really believe. If we say we love God, it's important to give Him our time. Any time is better than no time.

Time will never be wasted at an altar.

This isn't easy to talk about. We like to shove skeletons into the back of dark closets, walking away like the closet is empty. There is no corner where God can't see, and there is no darkness He can't light up.

When we read about Eden and the Fall, we tend to criticize the actions of Adam and Eve. *How could they? Why did they? Didn't they know?* Here's the hard truth: self-sufficiency is the false god that whispers lies about the true, sufficient goodness of God, and every day we have the choice to which one we will surrender.

Give into the god of self, believing the lie that within us are all the answers, or humbly walk with the real God who is the Light that shines on all things. All it takes is for someone to tell us that

God didn't mean what He said, and we bow our knees to the god of self.

Then if or when we return to God, and He breaks through to lift us up again, we ask those same questions. How could I? Why did I? Didn't I know?

Grace upon grace upon grace, sweet friend.

We will never be sufficient. Our ex boyfriends or girlfriends weren't sufficient. Our bosses are not sufficient. Not even our pastors, as anointed as they are, are sufficient. People can't save other people. We can't fill the cup of another endlessly, but we try and expect the same.

It's a path of brokenness because only God is sufficient. Only God can provide an endless supply of anything we need. Sufficient grace. Sufficient love. Sufficient hope. That's what is waiting in a Holy Moment with the Lord.

"Not that we are sufficient of ourselves to think any thing as of ourselves; but our sufficiency is of God." 2 Corinthians 3:5

Sufficiency. Wholeness. Healing. Where Holy can't be tainted, and everything left at the door is pardoned. Right in the middle of a Holy Moment.

"And he said unto me, My grace is sufficient for thee: for my strength is made perfect in weakness. Most gladly therefore will I rather glory in my infirmities, that the power of Christ may rest upon me." 2 Corinthians 12:9

Do you have visitors take off their shoes when they enter into your house? As a family, we take off our shoes, but we don't expect guests to. I give them grace. They don't live there. Still, each guest we have takes them off anyway.

The Lord placed this analogy on my mind about leaving self-sufficiency behind. I have found that most people who know they have dirty shoes, won't feel comfortable wearing them while visiting. Even if not asked, they will take them off at the door. As a sign of reverence to the person who lives there.

Self-sufficiency has to lay at the door of a Holy Moment. We have to surrender the tight grip it has on our feet and let it go because if we try to encounter God, thinking we are sufficient, we have bought again the first lie sold in the garden.

That we are equal to Holy. That we are like God. This, my friend, is the biggest lie ever sold.

What does leaving behind self-sufficiency look like? Not assuming you know God's answers to your questions. Praying *and* pausing. Embracing quiet to listen. Understanding He has things to say as well. Approaching Him with humility, knowing your position as a child of God.

Leaving behind self-sufficiency is believing you are His, which develops a reverence and a fearful disposition for the Creator of the Universe. It looks like less of you and more of Jesus. It's the posture of bowing down and looking up. Being silent and opening our ears to hear. Accepting the Lord knows what is best for us.

"Peter saith unto him, Thou shalt never wash my feet. Jesus answered him, If I wash thee not, thou hast no part with me." John 13:8

Right before The Lord Jesus Christ was betrayed and crucified on the cross at Calvary, He gathered a water pot and a basin to wash the feet of the disciples. The custom of the day was for water to be provided to traveling guests because their feet would be dirty. Not only was this an act of service but also an act of love. Jesus was demonstrating this in real time to those who chose to follow Him.

It was a Holy Moment.

When Holy was meeting with unholy.

Peter didn't understand. Confused, he watched the Messiah pour water over one foot after another, washing off the grime and wiping them with a towel. Then moving to the next person. Love in humble action.

I wonder what Peter was thinking as he watched Jesus bow to wash the feet of his fellow laborers. His Master, His God, His Savior. *Serving instead of being served.* Humbly making Himself low so that others could rise.

"He riseth from supper, and laid aside his garments; and took a towel, and girded himself. After that he poureth water into a bason, and began to wash the disciples' feet, and to wipe them with the towel wherewith he was girded. Then cometh he to Simon Peter: and Peter saith unto him, Lord, dost thou wash my feet? Jesus answered and said unto him, What I do thou knowest not now; but thou shalt know hereafter." John 13:4-7

The times where I approach God, thinking I already know what's happening or what He's doing, are when I typically encounter Him less. This is not because He's gone or unwilling. God is always present and willing to meet with us.

Yet He knows our hearts, and a heart that is already settled *without* coming to Jesus is a heart that is blinded by a god that cannot save.

The god of self-sufficiency. The false god of self.

Peter's *"You don't have to Lord, I can do it"* attitude is nothing new to us.

"*God, I can handle this on my own. You're my God, but I'm not going to bother you. I can handle it.*"

I was taught to stand up for yourself, work hard, and do what you need to do. While there is space for that, in specific contexts, there is no space for self-sufficiency at the feet of Jesus.

We must be willing to lay it down and leave it there. While Jesus is waiting to cleanse us and is in position to serve, we stand in self-sufficiency. Even if Peter was thinking he wasn't worthy of this expression of love from Jesus, this ultimately means Peter had defined what his own worth was on his own terms.

The pride that rose up within his heart exposed a truth that spilled out through his words. Peter's heart was as dirty as his feet. Denying a gift from the Lord Jesus Christ because *you* don't feel like you're worth it still focuses on YOU.

Yes, the gift is for our benefit, but Peter missed something. Let's not miss it, too. Our purpose in this life is to know God. To have a relationship with Him. This is what Jesus was building when He came to earth—His Kingdom through His children.

Beautiful connection fueled by love so that sin could be demolished and our souls restored back to a tranquil place with our Lord and Savior.

Jesus always wanted us. He defines our worth. We don't.

"Peter saith unto him, Thou shalt never wash my feet. Jesus answered him, If I wash thee not, thou hast no part with me." John 13:8

I put this verse twice because I want us to understand the tension in this scene. Peter was missing Jesus' purpose. He was so focused on being self-sufficient with false humility that he rejected the gift of intimacy.

Jesus was extending His service as a lesson, yes, but also as an extension of relationship, of His love. Did you know being intimate rarely has to do with sexual actions? I know that tends to be where our minds go when we read that word.

To be intimate is to be close with someone in a loving way. Simple as that. Not just with a spouse but also with our God.

Where do we think this desire for intimacy comes from? That longing need to connect and fellowship with someone else? If we are made in the image of God, this means our need for intimacy stems from a God who believes in relationships.

A Holy Moment is an intimate moment.

Jesus was being an example of a humble servant, of course, but He was also establishing His purpose in that moment: *to be known.*

Jesus wants us to intimately know Him. So, He positions Himself ready for intimate connection, patiently waiting for us to accept the invitation. He knelt, and washed, and served. It had nothing to do with any of them deserving it, but it had everything to do with the love of Jesus.

Judas had his feet washed by Jesus, too. The same Judas who walked with Christ one minute and who would betray Him the next. The same Judas who had a plan to hand over his Master for a few lousy coins.

If we think that Jesus washed the feet of the disciples because they earned it, we'd be dead wrong. None of them did, but the Lord blessed them anyway. Building a relationship means to show up with the intention to bless someone other than yourself. That's what Jesus did and continues to do every single day.

Dying to the god of self is the challenge because wherever we go, so does the god of self. I understand. It's hard. This is why I believe we need to talk about it. Often we are blinded by our own motives, and we feel our emotions are justified.

I'm sure Peter thought he was doing a great thing, refusing to let Jesus wash his feet. The subtle nature of the god of self is by design. It starts off soft and gentle where it seems harmless. As time goes on, it'll get bolder because it's never satisfied.

The god of self thrives off of lust and selfishness to which there are no limits either. Our flesh calls the shots, and our inner self obeys.

"Watch and pray, that ye enter not into temptation: the spirit indeed is willing, but the flesh is weak." Matthew 26:41

Daily devotion to God puts the god of self back in its rightful place. Quiet and submissive to the presence of the Lord.

"Seeing then that we have a great high priest, that is passed into the heavens, Jesus the Son of God, let us hold fast our profession. For we have not an high priest which cannot be touched with the feeling of our infirmities; but was in all points tempted like as we are, yet without sin. Let us therefore come boldly unto the throne of grace, that we may obtain mercy, and find grace to help in time of need."
Hebrews 4:14-16

The Lord is ready to wash more than just our feet. God of the universe, of the galaxies, and of every living thing on Earth. He still looks down and cares about our heart and our soul. He is a God of the individual.

Jesus is in position to have an intimate Holy Moment with you. If you're messy, He wants to cleanse you and not because it was earned. Holiness and righteousness is found in the presence of the Most Holy and the Most Righteous.

Rejecting this intimacy is rejecting your purpose.

Peter had to come to the real issue and see his error. In front of the other disciples, he laid down his prideful declaration and accepted the intimate invitation of Jesus.

I wonder what Peter thought, when just a little while after that moment, Jesus was on a cross, bleeding for the sins of the world and for every disciple whose feet were cleansed. Staring up at the face that was just bowed over a murky bowl.

Please, friend. Do not deny the intimacy of God, even if your reasoning seems justified. Our purpose is to know God. That can only happen if we sit and allow Him to cleanse us in the way that only He can.

4

Typing the word "intimacy" while writing about God is odd. We just don't tend to use that word when associating ourselves with the Lord. It can be uncomfortable for us, and so we reject it.

Rejection is very hurtful. Our past rejection conditions us not to easily trust. Rejection can make good people do not-so-good things in order to feel validated or valuable.

God is not like the person who rejected us.

Hagar was rejected and was cast aside so harshly. If she retaliated, she would have been justified according to our current societal beliefs.

Hagar could have used the humiliating rejection as fuel to keep God out and take matters into her own hands. Isn't that what we're told by the culture we live in today, especially as women?

You can be your own hero. You can be your own boss. You can shout, and yell, and bulldoze other people to make a way for yourself. Because you were rejected, and you deserve it. Go slay, queen!

When the world puffs up the god of self within you, it's a projection of the self-sufficiency awoken within them.

There is nothing wrong with being a strong woman as long as that strength comes from the Lord, and we're not trying to be the dominant gender or influence. *Dominance isn't holiness.* Yet many women allow rejection to harden them and label it strength when it's really unhealed pain.

I understand that rejection hurts. It's ugly. In our pain, we can feel powerful in our feelings, causing us to stand up and fight. The problem with this reaction is that we never know when to stop fighting. It keeps going and spills over into our devotion to God as believers.

We are on the defense so much that we don't put down our fists and lift up our chins.

Being rejected will take the wind out of our sails and the praises out of our mouths. Be encouraged! In a Holy Moment, God can bring breath back into you.

We all want to be accepted. We all want to feel good enough. When the door shuts in our faces, and harsh words are said, there is a bubble of anger that we want to hold as a souvenir of the disgrace we've endured. *Look at what they did!*

We were never created to hold heavy things.

The more we try to clench our grip on being justified, the more overwhelmed we will become. This begins a sad cycle of preserving our self-sufficiency instead of letting God fight for us.

Let's take a pause and think about things practically for a minute. You have been rejected. This could mean being ignored (again) at work, turned down by a crush, or people you have respect for don't respect you back. Ouch.

Scientists have now found evidence that our brains react to social rejection the same way it reacts to physical pain. Studies from Purdue University done in 2003 have shared results that confirm this truth.

When we are rejected, our brains show activity in the areas that are usually reserved for physical pain. No wonder children can have a hard time fitting in! They are feeling the rejection like a real wound. The mind records this pain the same.

What happens after we are rejected? What do we usually do? Typically we shut ourselves off as a way of protection. Maybe we've said, *"I'll never talk to her again!"* or, *"I won't cry over him."*

Being rejected hurts. It can be disheartening. It can be mean. Our reactive behavior is to go into ourselves. We retreat. We hermit. There is a wound that is painful, and we don't want to be exposed again. We put temporary band-aids over unhealed rejection.

It's an instinct to protect ourselves from future pain. We don't want to get hurt any more than we have been already. What we have to understand is our need to keep ourselves safe from pain usually isolates God from healing us. Not because He can't do it, but we must extend the invitation for Him to do it.

God will heal in His own timing. Not ours.

He will wait until we ask Him to come and be with us. In keeping rejection at arm's length and not giving into the vulnerability, we end up rejecting God. While we are reacting to the pain from people, the Lord is waiting to be with you right in the middle of it all.

Not feeling wanted or accepted is a terrible feeling, especially when you're showing up as your most authentic self, and someone doesn't like it.

It's tough. However, the moment we start treating God the way we were treated, that's the opposite of a Holy Moment. It's the unholy trying to control the moments alone for their own benefit.

What we must do is ask the Lord to help us recognize our unhealthy patterns with rejection, especially if it interferes with our faith. God wants nothing more than to see us spiritually healthy. We can't build faith by keeping Him at a distance. He is an intimate God whose purpose is to be known. Even when the rejection is too much for us to bear, keep in mind Jesus stretched His arms on the cross so you have someplace to run.

"Surely he hath borne our griefs, and carried our sorrows: yet we did esteem him stricken, smitten of God, and afflicted. But he was wounded for our transgressions, he was bruised for our iniquities: the chastisement of our peace was upon him; and with his stripes we are healed." Isaiah 53:4-5

The world treated The Lord Jesus Christ as unholy. Instead of embracing Who He had revealed Himself to be, the Father and the Messiah, they cut Him off, shutting out the only Voice that could speak life. They rejected the King.

If anyone knows about rejection, it's Jesus.

The same way the Lord showed up at Calvary, He shows us whenever we willingly go to Him. Yes, He is that good! *Jesus is that Holy.*

I pray that we would pause long enough, when we are tempted to reject Holy, and would choose to lean in instead. To lean into the Holy Spirit, even when we've been rejected, confused, pushed aside or hurt. That instead of allowing our emotions to envelope us, we would allow our Father to carry us through.

The only acceptable rejection is for us to reject our flesh. When we deny ourselves in order to pursue Holy, then rejection becomes the beginning of healing. Just think. What would have happened to Adam and Eve if they rejected their flesh? We would have a different world. Yet in the midst of the sinful agenda of the enemy, there's an intimate place where we can enter into the garden and be in the presence of our first Love.

"If any man will come after me, let him deny himself, and take up his cross daily, and follow me." Luke 9:23

As we approach Holy, we will need to leave behind unholy things. This may not be a surprise to you. You may have already been through multiple processes of repentance and purging. Such is the life of a born-again Christian. The process of rejecting self is continual because sin abounds still.

This is the first step to encountering a Holy Moment. Rejecting your natural urges to be self-sufficient. When our flesh has the urge not to connect with God, we must deny any thoughts or feelings that will try and tell us it's not worth it. Anytime we are tempted to reject the Lord, remember it is not a reflection on who He is. *Rejecting God has nothing to do with God.*

It has to do with two things: our own diluted perception about our value and how we've been treated in the past by people.

Our spirituality often pays the price for the wounds we have endured. We can't control what is done to us and the rejection that will happen. The one thing we can control is what we do with it afterwards when we are alone and no one else is around. Will we allow the rejection to stay with us? Or will we approach God so that in one Holy Moment, He can turn that rejection into triumph?

God's grace makes it possible for us to know who He is and opens the door to a deeper relationship with Him. His grace is His willingness to share with us His Identity. There's beauty in that connection that self-sufficiency can't mimic.

Jesus knows what we need when we don't feel good enough, and by His grace, we find what we need in Him. With God, we have enough.

5

Enough. So much weight is held in one word. How do we measure our *"enoughness"?* Can it even be measured? If we polled a group of teenagers in a youth group, they may have totally different answers than a group of senior saints. A senior saint is a faithful believer who has been through some storms in life and still shows up. Teenagers, though fun and spunky, typically don't have the same world view or experiences. Yet.

Enough can interrupt a Holy Moment with the Lord in one of two ways (or, let's be honest, both):

1. We think we are enough on our own, *and/or*

2. We say we're not good enough to be with God.

Both of these mindsets are founded on a false foundation of self-sufficiency.

The world feeds us the broken promise of fullness if we look within ourselves or out into the universe. This point of view is outside of God's will. When people are so convinced that they can be whole without the divine hand of their Creator, they will naturally act in a way that serves themselves.

It's about our focus. A person in pain will typically seek an antidote to gain relief. *This world is filled with temporary antidotes to spiritual problems.* Whether it's a pill or a person, we are marketed further away from seeking the Great Physician. In the middle of sugar-coated satisfaction, we pacify ourselves with an *"I'm enough"* stamp and try to move forward.

The truth is we never really move anywhere because the trap of saying *"I'm enough"* sends us down a dark rabbit hole of instability. Thinking we are healed when the wound is deeper than we can see. In our brokenness, God's heart breaks because His creation was never meant to seek wholeness outside of His presence.

Yet here we are. While Jesus beckons for us to return back to the garden where He is more than enough to heal everything. In the garden of Eden, needs were met thoroughly. The Lord didn't forget to give Adam and Eve anything. They had what they needed to be sustained and fulfilled to the max. It was when the focus turned inward as they were deceived into sin. When God being enough and doing enough was no longer enough for them.

The flip in perspective is where we need to look. Thinking we are enough doesn't give us motivation for devotion. Seeking God's face isn't a priority when we are full of ourselves. Even if our motives are genuine, they can still be wrong. This is where the concept of *enoughness* in the world falls flat when compared to the gospel.

Being genuine is not the same as being truthful. No matter how sincere we can be in our longing for answers, if we are not spending time with God and seeking after Him, whatever fruit is gained otherwise is rotten to the core.

"Beware of false prophets, which come to you in sheep's clothing, but inwardly they are ravening wolves. Ye shall know them by their fruits. Do men gather grapes of thorns, or figs of thistles? Even so every good tree bringeth forth good fruit; but a corrupt tree bringeth forth evil fruit. A good tree cannot bring forth evil fruit, neither can a corrupt tree bring forth good fruit. Every tree that bringeth not forth good fruit is hewn down, and cast into the fire. Wherefore by their fruits ye shall know them."
Matthew 7:15-20

Jesus was teaching an important lesson here in the sermon on the Mount. It is that we will know who a person is by the fruit they produce. Fruit would mean any evidence of how a person lives their life, which could be seen through their actions and words.

He knew that the religious people of the day would teach one thing but do the opposite. Jesus understood how much confusion that brought to the Jewish people.

We are not inherently good apart from Jesus no matter what is taught outside of the Word of God. Whatever good is produced in us and through us is by His grace. To God be the glory alone! The label of being "enough" waves a flag of vanity that points to us as savior.

In the beauty of God's grace, choosing to love unconditionally doesn't qualify us as enough. It has nothing to do with us. God loves each person through the layers of self-indulgent flesh. This speaks volumes of His unfailing mercy to see the soul. We can't do anything to separate us from that love.

The word "enough" means "to the extent." So when we say, *"I am enough,"* we are taking God out of the equation that only He Himself crafted. Your makeup of who you are as a human being, as a living soul, can only exist because of the Lord. Though He loves you, that doesn't erase your sin automatically. There's a process, and it includes reformatting how you approach Him.

"As it is written, There is none righteous, no, not one: There is none that understandeth, there is none that seeketh after God. They are all gone out of the way, they are together become unprofitable; there is none that doeth good, no, not one." Romans 3:10-12

As pure as we believe our motives to be, we are still sinful creatures standing on a planet that perfectly spins because of the One who made it. How could I look at the way nature works and think within myself is the full extent of all I need? This is not meant to be degrading. We are gaining a new perspective about being enough. There is not a chance that any created thing has the potential to be enough.

God has proved over and over again that He is enough, and even that word minimizes how great God truly is. The existence of life itself and our inherent value only comes from the Lord who gives life.

God sets the bar for enough. Not us.

I dare not look in the mirror and utter that *"I'm enough"* as a badge of honor for being chosen. Knowing full well salvation was due to a merciful, Holy God wanting to redeem us. We are chosen because of His grace. The Lord became flesh and died to save everyone according to His love, not according to our qualification.

We didn't deserve it because we're good. Definitely not because we're enough. God can't lie, and He cannot deny Himself, so therefore He loves. *This love is enough to save.* This doesn't speak one word about the quality of my character, but it sure echoes the quality of His.

**"It is a faithful saying: For if we be dead with him, we shall also live with him: If we suffer, we shall also reign with him: if we deny him, he also will deny us: If we believe not, yet he abideth faithful: he cannot deny himself."
2 Timothy 2:11-13**

Over the years this phrase has been a debate continually challenging belief systems. It has divided fellow believers, and I understand why. One main argument has been that in uttering the phrase *I'm enough*, it is saying that God *makes* us enough. I've heard it explained that they aren't trying to glorify themselves but are saying that His love is so good, it makes them enough in Him. *I'm enough for Jesus.*

This is an understandable sentiment, but the issue I find is in the half truth. We don't earn His love. That part is the Biblical fact. There is nothing we can do that can separate us from the love of God. There is no weapon hell has and no words devils can speak. Not one thing will stop the Lord from loving us all equally. God's love is not based on race, gender, skin color, or geographic location.

The love of the Lord Jesus Christ is available for everyone, everywhere at all times. It is not based on who we are but reflects who He is.

"For I am persuaded, that neither death, nor life, nor angels, nor principalities, nor powers, nor things present, nor things to come, Nor height, nor depth, nor any other creature, shall be able to separate us from the love of God, which is in Christ Jesus our Lord." Romans 8:38-39

Using God's love as a way to say we are complete to the full extent of our ability is still self-serving whether we mean it to be or not.

We need relief from damaging thought patterns, and I'm aware that the words *I'm enough* have a pull on people of faith trying to live in a faithless society.

On the path to more humility, we can become humiliated. *Time with God every day is not for us to see how great we are.* Allow the Lord to lift you up as you seek Him for fellowship, reprogramming your mind to approach devotion like the divine appointment that it is. You don't have to be enough for Jesus to be with you.

A Holy Moment speaks of His Holiness. Every room He inhabits elevates the atmosphere. There is no secret dark corner to the Lord. He sees every inch. Infinite wisdom from an Infinite Deity. God doesn't need help or relationship. There's not anything that can be added or taken away from the Omnipresent, Omnipotent King.

The magnificent truth is that though the Lord Jesus Christ doesn't need anything from us to function or exist, He wants us anyway. There is delight in our obedience and response. The Lord's delight is not a sign of weakness, it's a sign of love. True love delights in watching others flourish in the good things that are given. It's not blind admiration without correction either. Parents know this as well. We correct those we love who are making mistakes. I'm grateful God does this kindly.

There is no *enoughness* within our wretched flesh. It is when our eyes move from us to Him that we really know what, or Who, is truly enough.

"And he said unto me, My grace is sufficient for thee: for my strength is made perfect in weakness." 2 Corinthians 12:10

Walking in the garden with God, how could we think of ourselves? We would be in His presence, communicating with the same Voice that spoke light into existence. What's more, He's willing to spend time with you, too, as a chosen vessel to reflect His Identity from head to toe, brain to heart.

What a patient, loving, faithful God who chooses to have a relationship in spite of our weaknesses!

6

Isn't it interesting how the Lord provided everything for Adam in the garden, and He still assigned him a job? It has always fascinated me. God didn't have to put Adam to work. He provided enough to sustain him.

Perhaps because the Lord works and because we are made in His image, we should work, too. Maybe God knows that work builds respect for what we have and cultivates an honor of worship.

Adam's work in the garden was worship to God.

After the commandment to bear fruit within marriage, God gave Adam a job to do outside of himself: take care of the garden. This included not only the animals, both on land and sea, but the land itself. The ground his feet stood upon.

"And the Lord God took the man, and put him into the garden of Eden to dress it and to keep it." Genesis 2:15

To "dress it" meant to till the ground. To be a gardener with hands in the soil, deeply invested in the quality of the land. To "keep it" meant to guard the land. *Protect and maintain it.* Preserve.

Why would God tell man to be a guard over paradise? What would man need to protect in a place where the Lord's presence is present?

I'm sure there are practical reasons for this. Insects can infest the garden, and it was man's job to keep them under control. Maybe a very zealous, chunky hippo could wander and devour more of his fair share of greens. Hey, it's possible!

While I do believe there are practical reasons behind most things in the Bible, I'm not foolish to forget the spiritual reasons the Lord leaves as breadcrumbs for His children to nibble on as they read scripture.

When God put man in the garden and gave him a job, it was for two purposes:

Honor the dwelling place in His presence *and*

Watch over what He has created.

Dress and keep. Work the ground to make it acceptable for growth. Till it. Get it ready for seeds and then guard it. Make sure nothing taints the work you've done and corrupts the ground ready for new life.

This job was intended to give respect to the place where God's presence was abiding with Adam. *He was tasked with taking care of the environment.* Intimacy with the Lord is hands on. The Lord doesn't just want us to be receivers of His blessings and goodness. *He wants us involved.*

Our work is our worship but not to boast of ourselves. God involved Adam in the honoring process of the garden. Of the place where he abides with His Creator so that Adam may know God intimately as he worked.

This is about a Father who intentionally involves man into the work of tending to the garden. The success of growth and bearing fruit is more than tangible production. This work also prepares for growth between man and God.

He gave man a job to do in the garden as an expression of worship to Him. The job was not to make man feel good about himself, although that might be a byproduct. It wasn't to boost his ego or pride. The work was to honor the place where the Lord's presence was and watch over what He has created.

Worship can be exciting and exuberant, but it can also stem from a dedicated, faithful work ethic. We may automatically think about powerful songs during church where the singers kick off their shoes, and the drummer plays so fiercely, a fire ignites. That's fun, but it's not all that worship entails. *Worship is also what you do at home when no one else is around.*

It's when we wash the dishes because our family needs them and fill the fridge with yummy food because people need nourishment. Worship can be cleaning the toilet because, well, waste is part of life. It's not glamorous, but it matters.

Till the ground, then guard it. That's the work. That's worship.

How you use your hands and posture your heart. At church, home, your job, or school. What we do with our hands is important to our relationship with God. How we posture our heart determines what kind of growth we will have. Honoring where His presence dwells and watching over it so that the good things God wants to grow in us have a chance to bloom.

When we enter into a Holy Moment with God, we are invited to participate in this special kind of worship. As we talk to the Lord in prayer and seek His face, we abide in His presence to know Him and also abide to worship Him.

Can you please direct my hands, Lord, so that they may bring you honor?

Can you please reposition my heart, God, so that I may be alert as you move in my life?

Worship to the Lord doesn't always involve big emotions expressed in a big way. It's anything you do that brings Him honor.

"And whatsoever ye do, do it heartily, as to the Lord, and not unto men; Knowing that of the Lord ye shall receive the reward of the inheritance: for ye serve the Lord Christ." Colossians 3:23-24

When we are working, we are worshiping. This change in our perspective molds our hearts to be sensitive and in tune with God. There is beauty in worshiping with sincerity and generosity, not with a grudge or a bad attitude. It might not be work we like, but it's for His glory.

How we work can make or break our worship.

God isn't looking for workers who are only concerned with people *watching* them serve. God is looking for the ones who understand that work is more than what is seen.

"And when thou prayest, thou shalt not be as the hypocrites are: for they love to pray standing in the synagogues and in the corners

of the streets, that they may be seen of men. Verily I say unto you, They have their reward. But thou, when thou prayest, enter into thy closet, and when thou hast shut thy door, pray to thy Father which is in secret; and thy Father which seeth in secret shall reward thee openly." Matthew 6:5-6

Worship without devotion is work without the heart. We can't honor where His presence is if we don't make time to get into His presence. In addition, we can't guard so good things can grow if we aren't postured to face the right way. The work is the action that positions you to face towards God. That is part of the worship.

Are you consistently going into that secret place? Do you limit distractions? How are you handling the job as a laborer, Adam? When it's all done for that moment, what fruit are you bearing?

This is the not-so glamorous portion of worship. When the lights are off and the parking lot is empty. *How you work in private is a showcase of how you've kept the garden.*

Worship is wiping counters, wiping noses, brushing hair, making breakfast. Tilling the ground of your heart and home. Worship is getting to church, ready to assist, and participate. Worship is preparing a Sunday School lesson, refilling the tissue boxes, vacuuming the carpet, cleaning the bathrooms. Worship is gathering the snacks, brewing the coffee, arranging the centerpieces, organizing the song books. Worship is testing the sound system, unlocking the doors, and dusting cobwebs. Tilling the ground of your church and sanctuary.

Tilling the ground is the preparation. Guarding the ground is being present before the growth. Dress it and keep it.

This is also a Holy Moment.

When you worship with your work.

The secret place can be a location in your home, but it also is a state of mind. Guarding the ground has nothing to do with how good we are. God asked Adam to guard the ground not because he was perfect and knew it all. He asked man to guard the ground to give him a chance to worship God through service.

Keep it. Watch over creation.

This is how you can worship Me.

In the New Testament, Martha knew that serving was an important skill, and she was the best at it. It was her house where Jesus sat and taught in Luke 10. Taking care of guests is what any good host should do, but what happens when that house guest is the Messiah?

"Now it came to pass, as they went, that he entered into a certain village: and a certain woman named Martha received him into her house." Luke 10:38

She received Him. Such a beautiful statement. I don't want to overlook this. Most of us wonder why our spiritual life is dry, yet the door stays closed as Jesus waits on the other side.

I don't want to go about the day oblivious. I want to know when Jesus is near and let Him in.

How did Martha open the door? With excitement or with haste? Was she doing chores and noticed Him out of the corner of her eye? We don't know that detail, but scripture does say that Martha wasn't alone. She had a sister named Mary.

"And she had a sister called Mary, which also sat at Jesus' feet, and heard his word. But Martha was cumbered about much serving, and came to him, and said, Lord, dost thou not care that my sister hath left me to serve alone? bid her therefore that she help me." Luke 10:39-40

Poor Martha. She was doing her best to be a great hostess. Can you sympathize with her frustration? She was serving others, which is an honorable thing, but Martha allowed her work to be a distraction when Jesus was in the room.

"And Jesus answered and said unto her, Martha, Martha, thou art careful and troubled about

many things: But one thing is needful: and Mary hath chosen that good part, which shall not be taken away from her." Luke 10:41-42

Being attentive is being active. There's a flow between serving and listening. If we define our relationship with Jesus *only* by our performance, we are missing that good part—the part that is willing to sit and just be.

Actively listening to the Lord is part of the work.

This might sound contradictory, but it marries beautifully with the work and the worship we are called to do through Holy Moments. It wasn't that Mary wasn't active. Martha was upset that Mary was not active the way *she was*. Mary was an active listener. Sitting still. Being attentive.

That is part of the work that God has called us to do, too. Just because someone is not performing the way we are doesn't mean they are not active in the Kingdom of God. Taking a moment to listen to Jesus is part of being a laborer. He has all the knowledge and instructions we need to be successful workers in the Kingdom.

When we talk about worship through our work, we should also talk about not comparing our work to one another. Martha focused her work on service but not with the right motive. Mary focused her work on listening to Jesus while ignoring the workload of her sister.

Mary's motive was to listen and sit.

Martha's motive was to serve and move.

As a laborer of the Lord, we need both.

Are we trying to do the job that God has called us to do without listening to Him? If our work is worship, our hearts should be in the right place, and we should have the right motive. You might be wondering how we can listen and sit but also serve and move.

When we are in tune with the Spirit of the Lord and have a relationship with Him, our awareness of what is needed is heightened. When we spend time listening to God and sitting at His feet, we grow in wisdom. Then when it's time for us to serve and move, we understand how to do it with the right heart as God directs us.

I think this is why it's difficult for us to take time to have devotion with God because our lists are so tight. We can't fit Jesus into our schedules. Imagine Jesus sitting in your living room, pouring out goodness, but you have not found time to be an active listener. You have only made time by being an active worker. We need to be both an active listener AND an active worker to be effective in the Kingdom of God.

You may have had conversations with people who tell you they are listening, but they can't repeat back any of the words that you have told them. They were not actively listening. The words were just bouncing off their eardrums, and so they heard the sound of your voice but did not properly process the words.

God doesn't want that. He wants His words to penetrate our hearts so that we can be changed. Not for us to just *hear* His words but to actively listen to them. Process them. Take them to heart. Let them change us.

I don't believe that Jesus was upset about Martha working and serving. That is what we are called to do. However, Jesus said that Mary had chosen one thing, and I believe that that one thing was actively listening. Taking time *before* serving to hear what He has to say.

In order for us to have those Holy Moments in our lives, we need to make time to be with God. Make time to actively listen to Him. Hopefully our worship will not only be attached to our works but will be present in being still in His presence. That we will actively listen to what Jesus has to say before we actively serve.

I have two sons, and one of them aims to please us. However, they normally act in haste. Sometimes I will ask for them to go into a different part of the house to bring me an item, but they have already left my presence before I finish explaining where to find that item. It takes more time for them to complete the task, to complete the job because they did not wait to hear the rest of the instructions. They have to back track and listen to the full command first. Then go.

My son has a heart to serve but not a motive to actively listen *before* serving. He's a child and will learn this in time. The Lord has many people who want to help, and that is great. Like I try to tell my sweet, thoughtful boy: *"When you do not wait for me to tell you how to help, it's actually not helpful at all."*

Serving without listening takes more energy because you don't have all the facts. It makes the job harder to accomplish. With this in mind, if we are to worship with our work, it is of the utmost importance to actively listen to Jesus before we do the work. Otherwise we might miss a crucial element that He is trying to tell us.

Jesus knew how troubled Martha's heart was and how her serving was not done with the right motive. If Martha would have taken the time to sit down next to her sister Mary at His feet, she would have had her own personal Holy Moment that would have changed how she approached serving.

One thing is needful. Choose that one thing. Sit and be in the presence of the Lord. Let Him direct the way you work, and serve, and move. Be filled with wisdom and discernment. Give God your time and attention each day so that when you are in the middle of the busyness in this life, you've already heard the voice of the Lord. A solid truth to hold onto.

7

Sunflowers are my favorite flower. I've always had a dream to plant a sunflower field. A crop of perky, bright sunflowers gleaning in the sunshine. I want to walk among them, admiring their beauty every day of the season. At one point, I even ordered sunflower seeds from a website, hoping to plant them at my home. Unfortunately, I couldn't find a spot for my sunflower patch.

Our ground is not very forgiving with invasive tree roots springing up through the turf like the backs of scaly sea monsters. A brief experiment in my flower bed showed success. I was able to grow different sunflowers one spring, and that brought me so much joy. I loved them. Yet I really wanted a sunflower patch. Not one row in a garden bed. So, I kept the new seeds and waited, not sure what would expire first—the seeds or my dream of a sunflower patch. The seeds sat on the shelf in our cool basement, with all the potential of being great, as I waited.

Fast forward a few years, and in a whirlwind of circumstances, we purchased a couple of acres in a beautiful mountain town only a few hours away from home. The perfect distance for a weekend getaway for our family. We bought a camper and parked it on the land. There was fishing, campfires, kayaking, yard games, and lots of playing fetch with Sonic our Blue Heeler pup.

In the spring of 2023, something prompted me to pack the seeds as we were headed to our land to mow and enjoy an amazing weekend away. The dream of a sunflower field rose up within me again, and I walked the property with my boys. They were equally excited about this vision, too.

We talked about the best spot sunflowers could grow. Having a couple of acres, it was nice to have options, but I had to account for the shadows of the nearby trees that would cast where we planted. Finally we decided to plant only two rows of sunflower seeds just to see if they would take to the ground. Another experiment. Hopefully, another step towards a patch.

Having a lot of seeds doesn't automatically mean a lot of growth. Often, some seeds don't grow. The only guarantee given is their potential. You plant the seeds, water them, and wait. Sometimes nothing sprouts.

I knew the possibility of the seeds not growing was real. We have never planted anything on this land before. How do I know it's the right ground for them? Also, I did have the seeds for a long time before this. Were they still good?

I decided to try anyway. We cleared a little area right by the road. I love driving by sunflowers. How fun would it be to have my own that could give people joy as they passed by our land? The flowers would also be a nice marker to let us know we were at our land as we drove up the road.

I spent an entire afternoon on the ground, gloves on my hands and seeds by my side. Raking, digging, planting, repeat. Having a dream is nice, but there's work to do, too.

I kept thinking about my first experiment back home in my garden bed. The most gigantic sunflowers grew to about six feet tall! There were also dainty ones, orange ones, and ombre yellow ones. They all grew well, and we loved them that year. Yet my heart wanted a patch, and this land was my only hope of that dream coming to life.

Motivated, I planted my little two rows and waited. I was full of hope and promise. Would those seeds take and sprout? I wouldn't know until we came back again. The next few weeks were torture. I didn't know how the weather affected the ground, if the soil was good, or if the seeds took.

When we plant, we do so with faith that whatever is needed for growth will come. It's a difficult thing to do when we're gardening, but it's also difficult to do in life as a believer. We are not God. We are not all-knowing. Yet we are called to follow and obey and trust the process. Plant with faith that growth will happen.

Letting go of control when you realize there's nothing you can do about a situation is hard. That's just the fact. The Lord Jesus Christ is able to provide everything seeds need to grow. Our role typically is to plant and pray.

Often, we want to get our hands dirtier and do more than we've been called to do. When we work with new souls or just our old sinful selves, planting in faith and praying with expectation is good. Trying to force growth when the ground isn't ready doesn't bring the results if there are any results at all.

My dream of a sunflower patch can be associated with harvesting of souls. There is a vision, and there is potential. We put in the work and do what we can—what God has asked us to do. Then we must let go of control and hope for the best outcome, trusting Him with the increase.

"So then neither is he that planteth any thing, neither he that watereth; but God that giveth the increase." 1 Corinthians 3:7

Paul wrote to the church at Corinth his concerns about their divisions and envying. He wanted to remind them that we are all laborers in Christ and that no soul belongs to us individually. It's a very beautiful (and convicting) point of scripture. I encourage you to study seeds, plants, and harvesting in the Word of God. It would change how you witness to people about Jesus.

In our western church culture, we pride ourselves as "soul winners," claiming this badge of honor as if we have the power to save anyone. As witnesses for the Lord Jesus Christ, we are to be a light in this dark world. We are to proclaim truth, teach Bible studies, and disciple those who truly want to know the Lord more intimately. To "win" means to draw or fetch souls—people for God. Yet the action of "soul winning" belongs to God alone.

We are the tool in the hand of the Gardener doing only what He has asked us to do. The increase, the revival, the saving of a life is His doing. You and I are merrily being used to reach out, plant, and water. God brings the growth.

"The fruit of the righteous is a tree of life; and he that winneth souls is wise." Proverbs 11:30

To bring someone to encounter their own personal Holy Moment with the Lord is an honor. God calls us to show souls the way to the Living Water, the Bread of Life. It is not, and never will be, within mankind to produce the power of growth spiritually. Only God alone has that power.

The Lord sees what we have planted in faith and hears our prayers for growth. No one else can. He has chosen to bless whomever He has chosen to bless.

As the God of all creation and the Maker of Heaven and Earth, the Lord has every right to grow those of us who have planted in faith. In our Holy Moments, we become content because we can trust the One who always meets us.

I'm happy to report that since writing this book, I have gone back to our land and checked on my seedlings. They sprouted beautifully! I choked up and almost cried on the side of that quiet road. A spring of joy flooded my heart. It caught me by surprise how emotional I was over sunflowers!

That's when I knew this was not about sunflowers. This was about a dream that I had tucked away within myself for so long, finally seeing that it was possible. I planted in faith and prayed for growth. Then, I saw it being fulfilled.

I'm not going to sit here and tell you that your dreams are going to come to pass because I can't predict that. I can't give you false hope when I don't know the details of your dream. The Lord knows all things. He knows what's best for us more than we do. It's possible that our dreams could be harmful to us. He knows what would happen if we truly got what we asked for. God wants us to seek something more than a dream. He wants us to seek Him, and if we can be content with seeking Him even when we haven't received what we've desired, it's enough.

God is enough because God is the dream.

A real, loving relationship with the Creator of the world where we are walking with Him daily and He with us. Where Holy Moments are woven into our everyday lives because we are tethered to the God of eternity. His hand over us, on us, and working through us. What a dream that is!

When we are waiting for what we want most or what we think we need, I hope we don't miss the main focus. We need to seek the Lord Jesus more than the results we want. We should ask ourselves serious, honest questions. Will my relationship with God change if my prayer comes true? Am I spiritually mature enough to give Him the glory? If the Lord decided to never fulfill my dream, is He still good?

Sit with these questions. Be real with yourself. God knows the ins and the outs of who we are. What He has given us is sufficient because He is sufficient. The lover of widows and the fatherless. An Advocate for the least of these.

Move to be content with whatever God has given you to steward in this moment right now. Treat it well. Allow the expectations for the future to sit in the garden with the Gardener.

The sunflowers for me was a metaphor for other things in my life. They represented a healthy marriage. A loving family. To be a writer. To be an artist. To preach the gospel. To be used in mighty ways. To have children and be a happy mom.

All of those were dreams way before my tangible sunflowers. As I stood and watched the sprouts and felt such joy, that's when I saw how Jesus had fulfilled all those life dreams I had. The ones I whispered to Him in our Holy Moments.

Growth is always possible. Miracles are always possible. God always does new things and is always creating new life, even if that means the life of a dream. As you are waiting, plant in faith and pray with expectation. Seek the Maker first above all things. Allow Him to sprout new things within you that will strengthen your spiritual life.

No matter what the results are in the end, you have a Solid Rock on which you can stand. You are tethered to something that is not bound by the ground. You are tethered to the Lord of lords and the King of kings.

You are tethered to Jesus—the real Dream.

8

Influence in the garden was evident. When Adam and Eve thought they weren't being noticed by God, their posture changed. One entered into sin, and the other followed. Obedience to God can be contagious, but disobedience also has the same effect. Influence is two-fold.

I confess there was a time when I was afraid of going too deep with God because it meant other people wouldn't be coming with me. More life in Christ meant relational deaths I wasn't ready to grieve. Giving the Lord more of my time meant more changes in me, and my awareness of those I hung around would strengthen.

That would mean some people wouldn't be ready to join me in the garden experience with God. Aren't we like that? To tie ourselves to one another as dependents as faith hangs in the balance.

It reminds me of the story where Jesus enters into a garden before giving His life to be crucified. He doesn't go alone, but He brings a select few with Him. Jesus presented an opportunity for these disciples to humble themselves and to watch and experience a Holy Moment with God.

"And they came to a place which was named Gethsemane: and he saith to his disciples, Sit ye here, while I shall pray. And he taketh with him Peter and James and John, and began to be sore amazed, and to be very heavy; And saith unto them, My soul is exceeding sorrowful unto death: tarry ye here, and watch." Mark 14:32-34

By joining Jesus in the garden of Gethsemane, the three disciples were given a glimpse into a Holy Moment. As the time was approaching for the Lord Jesus Christ to sacrifice His body on the cross, He entered into a garden to prepare the flesh for what was to come. If we enter into a Holy Moment regularly, it'll prepare us before the difficult and brutal trials of life.

The Lord Jesus Christ has no sin, but as a man, He felt the pull of His humanity and was tempted. Just like us. Just like Adam and Eve. We have a God who understands what it feels like to be tempted. Who knows firsthand the struggles of the flesh. This is why before the cross, He took time in a garden.

"And he said, Abba, Father, all things are possible unto thee; take away this cup from me: nevertheless not what I will, but what thou wilt." Mark 14:36

From our perspective, it would seem as though the cross was the main obstacle. We would be terrified of something so horrific. Being nailed to wooden planks half alive, hanging, and suffering until our organs began to fail.

Yet when we read the context of Jesus in the garden in Mark's account of what happened before the crucifixion and His mental state, it reveals that the main obstacle for the Lord Jesus Christ was His will as a man.

The cross was not the final challenge. The Lord has all power to defeat death and sin. He was very much still fully God as He operated as fully man. Though He had placed limitations on Himself when He came to earth, Jesus was God. **That never changed. It's who He is.**

He is the God who reigns above all creation and who made the stars. The God declared to be the First and the Last, the Alpha and Omega. The Almighty. The God who operates alone and shares His glory with no one else. *This God became flesh.*

In His earthly body, there was a wrestling that we can relate to. The tug between the flesh and the spirit. As a man, the real challenge was His human will.

In Matthew's account, he words this tension in a way I can appreciate. As Jesus was in the garden of Gethsemane, after praying in agony and sorrow, He notices the disciples sleeping. His heart is stirred, and He says this:

"Watch and pray, that ye enter not into temptation: the spirit indeed is willing, but the flesh is weak." Matthew 26:41

The core of our human nature is selfish by default. Jesus recognized this. The weakness of our human flesh is that it does not want to submit to another authority. It wants to reign supreme. The disciples sleeping in the garden as Jesus is praying fervently, and denying His will as a man, is an illustration of how easy it is for us to treat the Holy Moments as mundane obligations.

This is not an attack on rest. I'm a huge advocate for proper rest, specifically when it comes to the things of the Spirit. I believe we who follow Christ should prioritize rest the way He did. This doesn't always mean sleeping. Although that kind of rest is needed and appreciated.

The disciples sleeping in the garden after Jesus told them to watch is where the error is. He wanted them to learn from this Holy Moment. There were rich lessons waiting on the other side of their heavy eyelids. Our bodies are going to crave certain things, and some of those things aren't bad. Rest and sleep aren't bad. The issue is in the disobedience of the command.

"...tarry ye here, and watch." Mark 14:34b

Tarry means to remain and be present. Jesus was saying, "Be here *with* me," followed by, "Watch." Stay awake. Be vigilant and alert.

Imagine the Lord in the flesh inviting you to take part of such a vulnerable, intimate experience. Not for His benefit, but for yours. Watching as He prays and is honest about His feelings. Hearing the anguish and seeing the heavy tears fall. The Lord of lords, the King of kings, on His knees in humble surrender in the middle of a garden.

I wonder what the smell of the air was like. Was the evening mist full of fog, the grass with beads of glistening dew? Was the scent fresh? Were there fluttering insects or birds overhead?

Did nature understand its Creator was now bowed on the earth He made, weeping for the sins of the world? As the Lord Jesus Christ cast aside His will as a man, did nature watch as the disciples slept? Imagine if they had, knowing their very existence was in the palm of His hand.

We were created differently than the animals and all of nature. We were made in His image and likeness. Given grace through free will, an unwarranted olive branch of love. The flesh is indeed weak, but there is still hope in the spirit.

Our humanity doesn't have to dictate our destiny. There is still time to awake and rise. To lay down our will for the will of the One who laid down everything for us. There is temptation to be distracted by the chaos in the world where the root is a global sin epidemic. Pray for the world, but pray more for His will over your soul.

What pulls on our hearts and causes us to slumber when we've been invited to tarry and watch? Your influence on the world starts here.

"The thief cometh not, but for to steal, and to kill, and to destroy: I am come that they might have life, and that they might have it more abundantly." John 10:10

Jesus was an example in the garden that day. No matter what we face, His will is sufficient. How could we, knowing what Christ gave up that day, look in the mirror and think we can live life abundantly without Him? There is no abundant life without Jesus.

It is the act of self-surrender that truly leads to an abundant life with our Savior.

The invitation to sit in the garden with Jesus is a beautiful illustration of His love for His children. *Watch me surrender so that you may know how to do the same. Be still and be with me.*

Life is full of different seasons. There are the mountain-top moments and the deep valleys. It's clear in the Word that God shows up in them all.

To accept the garden invitation is to choose His way over your own. When we enter into a Holy Moment with the Lord, we become examples to others the way Christ was an example to us. Our obedience to His will contributes to raising the bar of their faith.

It may not seem like much on the outside. Seeds take time to settle, and time will reveal the fruit of the planted influence. We may not be responsible or in control of the outcome. It's not love to force someone to enter their own Holy Moment with God.

As we enter into the rest of the garden and continually obey the still, small voice of the Lord, we will be an example of faithfulness to those watching our journey. A light set on a hill. The more we spend time with God, the more His love will shine through us. A glimmer of hope to the hopeless. A spark of victory for the weary. A beam of peace to those in need of revelation and true rest.

I didn't realize when I focused on the commitment of others that I allowed the quality of my faith to stay low. I gave my flesh permission to sleep as I watched others slip away around me.

Where we set the bar of our faith will either lower or raise the bar within the faith of someone else. When we allow ourselves to encounter consistent Holy Moments with God, by our example, it shows others they can also walk in the garden with Him.

This is not a competition between us—between me and you. This is a competition between our will and His. Between our flesh and His grace. Every day, we have the opportunity to lay ourselves down in an act of self-sacrifice over being self-sufficient.

In the garden, temptation found Adam and Eve. Yet, it was in a garden where God in the flesh resisted temptation and surrendered.

Tarry and watch. There is an invitation to sit in the garden with Jesus. He's waiting for you.

9

As I'm writing the tail end of this book, it's raining outside once again. The entire month has been a soggy mess with colder temperatures than I would like. Besides my own discomfort and longing for sunnier days, I have noticed the impact that too much rain has on the outdoors.

Plants have been waterlogged with saturated roots and no new growth. Any wooden structures are prone to soggy rot, their color darkened by the moisture. Stepping through the yard kicks up sloppy mud. There hasn't been a rest from the downpour of rain water in weeks.

In the Bible, the first garden was created with the right amount of what was necessary. Without the proper balance of sun and hydration, life in a garden would be unbearable. In fact, the Lord had a river that flowed from Eden out to other parts of the earth. In Eden, both the natural water source and the Living Water were present.

"And a river went out of Eden to water the garden; and from thence it was parted, and became into four heads." Genesis 2:10

I'm not going to sugarcoat it. Being in a dry, desert place spiritually is one of the loneliest experiences any human being can go through. I might be complaining about the excessive rain water in the natural world right now, but I know it would be equally as disturbing to have no water at all. Not a drop to nourish the parched land.

Years ago, a very important relationship to me was strained. I use that term loosely as it was more complicated and serious than that. This connection was once exciting until it wasn't. The conversations had more desolate moments with increasing tension as time went on.

We became stuck in a cycle of intense strife. Sometimes over simple things. I could feel the relationship slipping away like sand in my hands, and so, I closed them. Tightly. Out of fear that if I didn't take control, the wind would blow, and they would be gone forever.

This is not a dramatic statement. It was undoubtedly the truth in how I felt and behaved. In my words, I thought I was giving life when I was actually stifling it. Trying to fix and micromanage our relationship. A self-appointed crisis control agent, pointing out flaws in the communication, in their demeanor, and the overall spiritual health of what was brought to the table.

It was exhausting, even though I couldn't admit it. For the both of us. I had positioned myself as the arbitrator of truth and them as the meager student who should receive correction without complaint. Of course, that didn't work.

I believed the lie that on my own, I could be strong enough to stand in the middle of the desert. Positioning my performance as a token for His grace and expecting others to pay up the same way. *Grace from me wasn't free.* It came with strings. I became entangled in a web of selfish motives where my righteousness was justified. After all, I know God. I could handle anything.

This seed of self-righteous control bloomed and spiraled. There was no joy—only judgment. Past wounds were used as blockades. I was not going to let them hurt me, not going to allow discouragement of any kind, and not going to let bad things happen in life. What sounded like bravery to me was really fear in disguise.

Then God sent someone with a message for me. It was unexpected, and I was blindsided. It shook me to my core. How could I be in the wrong when I was trying to *do* everything right? How was this fair? Am I really that terrible of a person that God would send someone with a Word for me?

There it was. Springing up out of the depth. This was confirmation that the messenger was whom the Lord indeed sent to speak to my sorry soul trapped in a weary desert place. All of my actions couldn't hide the fragile ego just under the surface. Self-importance holding hands with pride. I shattered like a broken mirror from the inside out.

There is nothing wrong with working on a damaged relationship. Unless we believe the only sustainable water source is within ourselves.

"There is a way which seemeth right unto a man, but the end thereof are the ways of death. Even in laughter the heart is sorrowful; and the end of that mirth is heaviness. The backslider in heart shall be filled with his own ways: and a good man shall be satisfied from himself." Proverbs 14:12-14

Solomon wrote about a "backslider in heart." Someone who thinks their own ways are right. When we see this term used in modern Christian circles, we have a vision of someone running away from God. Leaving behind the life of a believer and going into the world with open arms.

This illustration is of a person who has put trust into their own ways. A person who is content in their actions and justifies them in their heart. We don't always read scripture and apply it to ourselves, but we tend to apply it more to others.

The Lord told my messenger that God didn't want my performance. *He just wanted me.* That in order for change to happen, I had to understand this. I was expecting top performance in exchange for love when God didn't. He just loves without what we can do. It is in that grace where we see the heart of the Lord and how we are supposed to be loving to one another.

Actions do matter, this is true. However, our actions don't change His commitment to love unconditionally. It just exists, and He gives us an invitation to abide within that umbrella of safety.

It's going to be a lifelong commitment of reflection and repentance, but I've already felt the shift. God is healing me more in every Holy Moment. Like Eve in Eden, the whisper turned into a false belief. The fragile concept that inside of myself, I had what would sustain and protect everyone. I wept bitterly for a long time. Fasting and praying about the message I was given, knowing without a doubt that it was from the Lord.

Not long afterwards during a Holy Moment, I wrestled with this profound revelation. Jesus sweetly stopped me. It was a supernatural quieting of my spirit as Holy met with unholy. An impressionable voice spoke to my heart:

You are not the Living Water. I am.

Do you know what it does to a dry spirit when the Word of the Lord speaks to it? It's like a bucket being dropped into a well. *Grace is coming.* The possibility for replenishment is coming. Hope to the weary, wounded, desert places is coming. From the only Living Water.

"And the Lord shall guide thee continually, and satisfy thy soul in drought, and make fat thy bones: and thou shalt be like a watered garden, and like a spring of water, whose waters fail not." Isaiah 58:11

Even in my sorrow, I was selfish. I couldn't see His grace clearly at all. Until the Lord spoke those words to my spirit, and the scales fell off.

With clarity from above, I began to see the big picture.

You are not the Living Water. I am.

A statement, not a question. A redirect, a turning away from a wide path unto a narrow way. The only narrow Way. It was a declaration that pierced my soul and left me speechless. When God speaks, there's no arguing. His Word will not return void but will accomplish what it's made to do. That day, it was to save me from myself.

I had adopted an idol of self, sitting on the throne where God should have been. I tried to control every aspect and person in my life, working hard to set the right environment or correct every wrong behavior, thinking I knew what was needed and how to do it all.

How could a flawed, imperfect human being be both the problem and the solution? We can't.

We all sin, which means making choices opposite of God's will for us. I was no exception to this, but I acted like the exception. I thought I was the solution, even though I was also the problem.

"In the last day, that great day of the feast, Jesus stood and cried, saying, If any man thirst, let him come unto me, and drink. He that believeth on me, as the scripture hath said, out of his belly shall flow rivers of living water." John 7:37-38

Jesus said that for those who believe on Him, out of His belly shall flow rivers of living water. We are a vessel that is poured into from Him above to nourish others. Flowing in and flowing out.

Living water doesn't begin within us. It doesn't start with us. Living Water is God and starts with Him. Humans can't be the solution to the problems. If that were true, the cross would be unnecessary. A vessel doesn't have the ability to fill itself and continually pour out.

The world tells us to be stronger, louder, and speak our truth. We're encouraged to be our own gods. It has led generations without the flow of the Living Water. Desperate and thirsty, trying to quench a desire that only God can provide.

Now I understand. I was trying to be the living water, but I am not God. I couldn't provide what only He can. No amount of performance was going to change that fact. The power of change and sustainability comes from a righteous God who works in pure and holy ways.

"And he shall be like a tree planted by the rivers of water, that bringeth forth his fruit in his season; his leaf also shall not wither; and whatsoever he doeth shall prosper." Psalms 1:3

We are not to be the living water but to plant ourselves beside the Living Water like a tree—steady and solid. Not moving when it gets uncomfortable but trusting that the Living Water will provide all that is needed in time of need.

By recommitting ourselves to private devotion with the Lord and showing up for those life altering Holy Moments, we will become the steadfast trees planted by the Living Water. Sustained and nourished by His Word that will flow into us and eventually through us.

10

When I was first saved, a wonderful woman at church began a Bible study with me. Over time, this woman became my mentor, friend, and eventually, my mother-in-law. I fell in love with our Bible studies and digging into the Word. I couldn't get enough as I began to privately study. Soon, I was teaching others what I had learned.

There's no greater feeling than showing someone the scripture, who Jesus is, and what He did for us. The gospel is still relevant and powerful. It's a beautiful witness to have the freedom to testify about the Lord and take time to explain why He's so wonderful.

It's something to keep in mind when we're struggling with our devotion time. A Holy Moment with God will prepare you to share God with others so that they can have their own Holy Moments. You will be a walking testimony that shines for Him. What an honor!

Recently, I lost a sister in Christ who was that walking testimony to me many times during my darkest days. She raised the most beautiful, godly young ladies in the truth. This book is dedicated to the four of them. Her life was a gift to many, and in her passing, her legacy continues to leave an impact.

Holy Moments don't go with us but live on in the lives that we touch.

Life is too fleeting to not include God in our time here on this side of Heaven. We can have all the birthday moments, party moments, graduation moments, parenting winning moments, new job moments, cherished married moments, retirement moments. *And they can be all good.* But without Holy Moments, none of the other moments matter.

The Lord Jesus Christ was led away from the garden of Gethsemane to face a trial and a cross. There was a reason Jesus asked His disciples to tarry and watch as He prayed. He was telling them: *This is a Holy Moment. You will need what is revealed here to sustain you soon.*

The sacrifice of the Lord Jesus Christ defeated death and sin once and for all. The pure blood of the Lamb of God poured out for us. The veil in the temple was torn, opening a new level of intimacy. *God with us. God in us.*

"Jesus, when he had cried again with a loud voice, yielded up the ghost. And, behold, the veil of the temple was rent in twain from the top to the bottom; and the earth did quake, and the rocks rent." Matthew 27:50-51

In the Old Testament, Moses' brother Aaron was the priest who made an atonement for the people. He was chosen to offer the needed animal sacrifices to cleanse God's people from their sin. This was a requirement for generations. Many priests came and went, fulfilling this holy job. *Until the day Jesus became that final sacrifice.*

Our God becoming flesh and dying on the cross means that the veil is no longer needed. We don't need a separation from Holy.

When Jesus died that day, the Bible says the veil "rent in twain from top to bottom," meaning it split in two. Think about how God's people must've felt when they watched that veil in the temple just tear wide open, exposing the Most Holy Place. Imagine it.

The precious blood of the Lord Jesus Christ reopening the Eden experience for us to dwell.

B. Meyer Commentary said it beautifully:

"With hushed hearts we stand in the presence of "that sight." It is the tragedy of time; the one supreme act of self-surrender; the unique unapproachable sacrifice and satisfaction for the sins of the whole world. It is here that myriads of sin-sick, terror-stricken souls, in every century, have found refuge."

The tearing of the temple veil breaks the division between the Most Holy and the unholy. It established a new covenant not seen or experienced before.

Between the High Priest and whoever will come.

His Spirit will not be kept behind a veil. It will not be contained but poured out upon ALL flesh! With the gift of the indwelling Spirit of God by evidence of speaking in other tongues, the Lord will abide within His people.

"And ye shall know that I am in the midst of Israel, and that I am the Lord your God, and none else: and my people shall never be ashamed. And it shall come to pass afterward, that I will pour out my spirit upon all flesh; and your sons and your daughters shall prophesy, your old men shall dream dreams, your young men shall see visions: And also upon the servants and upon the handmaids in those days will I pour out my spirit." Joel 2:27-29

A new covenant like no other. Where we can walk and talk with God as He dwells in us. Temples of the Holy Ghost. Living testimonies of His goodness and grace. That we may shine in a dark world, sharing the love of Christ with those in need of a Holy Moment.

"Having therefore, brethren, boldness to enter into the holiest by the blood of Jesus, By a new and living way, which he hath consecrated for us, through the veil, that is to say, his flesh; And having an high priest over the house of God; Let us draw near with a true heart in full assurance of faith, having our hearts sprinkled from an evil conscience, and our bodies washed with pure water." Hebrews 10:19-22

Aren't you thankful there is a new and living way? Our High Priest wants to spend time with us. We didn't earn it. It's proof of His everlasting love.

The separation is replaced by an invitation.

God is our salvation, our Redeemer, our Provider, and our Righteousness. To be righteous is to be morally right and just. That can only be the Lord. There is none Holy but Him. In that truth, we are given grace to approach from anywhere and, with liberation, to seek the face of our Creator.

The Lord is the Potter, and we are the clay. When we try to take full control, it's like the clay ignoring the hands of its Maker. Forgetting that in a moment, we can fall and shatter. We didn't make ourselves.

"Surely your turning of things upside down shall be esteemed as the potter's clay: for shall the work say of him that made it, He made me not? or shall the thing framed say of him that framed it, He had no understanding?" Isaiah 29:16

The Potter sees all things and knows how to heal brokenness. The grace He gives is undeserved. Taking time daily to accept the call to humility and the laying down of self-sufficiency is what a Holy Moment is about. *Having a moment with Holy.* The only Righteous one.

The Lord is my righteousness. Only God can mend, build, restore, renew. He is the Living Water that fills the holes spiritually within us, providing endless nourishment that will never run dry.

The Almighty God can form us into who we need to be, covering up the cracks from the past with His nail-pierced hands and holding us close. *The intimacy of Eden is still available today.*

"But now, O Lord, thou art our father; we are the clay, and thou our potter; and we all are the work of thy hand." Isaiah 64:8

When you experience pain and suffering as a Christian, God is digging a deep well within you. When a potter forms an open vessel, he fortifies the walls to make way for a center that will receive substance. A cup holds liquid. A vase holds a plant.

This internal well in you will hold anointing.

The deeper the well, the deeper the suffering. Hard ground can't be broken without digging and hard work. With every blow, it might feel like a setback. When you stay in the garden with the Holy One, He will carve space for an overflow of fresh anointing. The oil poured from the Potter into the center of your being.

The Lord is our Living Water. He will provide all that we need. If we stay close, God will use what hurt us to keep chipping away at that internal well. The deeper we go with God, the deeper the well is dug. The more obedient we are to the Lord and His Word, the more oil will be poured into the well to nourish us and others.

"To appoint unto them that mourn in Zion, to give unto them beauty for ashes, the oil of joy for mourning, the garment of praise for the spirit of heaviness; that they might be called trees of righteousness, the planting of the Lord, that he might be glorified." Isaiah 61:3

In the middle of a Holy Moment, God can turn ashes into beauty! Replace the mourning and sorrow with the oil of joy. Take the spirit of heaviness as you are robed with the garment of praise. The Almighty Father calls those who are faithfully planted trees of righteousness that He might be glorified.

You are the planted of the Lord!

Don't do it for the well. Don't do it for the oil. Those are both by-products of sticking close to the Living Water. *Do it for the Lord, and He will take care of it.* As you draw near to God and He to you, it will all be used to bring the King glory.

The well and the oil will benefit you. It will benefit those you love and are a witness to, but more than that, the well and the oil are examples of the depth and power of the Lord Jesus Christ.

Surrender to Holy Moments to be full of Him.

I want to be open to receiving all that God has for me, but I can't let His blessings be my motivation. They spark my gratitude, but the well and the oil together remind me of Who is really in control of this little thing called life.

It's never been me. Every day when I make the choice to surrender to a Holy Moment and enter into His presence, I want to remember that. **Jesus, be the center of this garden experience.** Be the center of my world. All blessings and sustainable resources flow from You forever.

"But seek ye first the kingdom of God, and his righteousness; and all these things shall be added unto you." Matthew 6:33

The Kingdom of God is wherever He is King. Is He the King within your life? Are you seeking His Righteousness alone?

It is time for every soul to commit or recommit themselves to the Lord Jesus Christ. He allows unholy to dwell and abide in His presence. While we still have the grace to do so, let us fully submit. Tomorrow is not a guarantee. Your influence in this fragile world shouldn't hang on a fragile faith. Whatever you have to sacrifice to enter into the garden with Jesus, do it.

This is my prayer as you go forth into the rest of your days. That you will recognize the need for deeper devotion, knowing each trial contributes to an anointed well within you. That Jesus is the True Living Water, the Sustainer of all we need. And that more Holy Moments lead to less of you and more of the Holy One. Amen.

Jacy Lee Pulford has authored and self-published a library of devotions, study guides, and coloring books for all ages. Visit the link below for more details.

https://linktr.ee/helloawesomelive

www.ingramcontent.com/pod-product-compliance
Lightning Source LLC
LaVergne TN
LVHW051523070426
835507LV00023B/3273